MW00465853

low fat
cooking

Published by:
TYPHOON MEDIA CORPORATION

low fat
cooking

Low Fat Cooking
© TYPHOON MEDIA CORPORATION

Publisher
Simon St. John Bailey

Editor-in-chief
Susan Knightley

Prepress
Precision Prep & Press

Includes Index
ISBN 9781582796543
UPC 615269965481

2010

Printed in The United States

introduction

The new gastronomical trends are imposing a lighter cuisine, with less cream, fewer saturated fats and quicker or steamed methods. There are reasons that, going beyond bodily aesthetics, justify the reduction in the consumption of animal fats. Cutting down on fried food, sugar, cakes and

pastry is important to avoid the raising of the so feared and widespread cholesterol. But lowering the level of fat in dishes does not mean that they should be boring. Or that if one person is on a diet, the whole family should not be able to follow it. We are what we eat; a healthier diet will improve and strengthen our whole body, and, consequently, will also enhance our physical appearance.

What has to be eliminated or reduced?

- Meat, poultry and fish will be replaced by their leaner equivalents.
- Egg yolks (highly cholesterolemid) will be reduced or eliminated, and replaced by egg whites (very proteid and fat-free).
- As for cheese and other dairy products, low fat ones will be preferred.
- Butter will be replaced by olive or sunflower oil.
- Instead of cream, it is preferable to use low fat plain yogurt (sugar-free).

- Tofu (soybean cheese) is a good base for sauces, fillings or salads. It is a good substitution for cream cheese because it adapts to any flavor and immediately absorbs the aroma of any seasoning that is added.
- Dressings, spices and herbs are essential to add flavor to the food, thus avoiding healthy but wearisome food.

If one wants to slim

It is better to see a nutrition specialist. But, as a rule:

- a normal adult requires between 1800 and 2500 calories a day;
- diet should vary according to individual factors such as age, sex and activity;
- physical exercise is the ideal complement of diet.

Difficulty scale

■□□ I Easy to do

■■□ I Requires attention

■■■ I Requires experience

chili
noodle salad

■□□ I Cooking time: 0 minutes - Preparation time: 35 minutes

ingredients

> **100 g/3¹/2 oz rice vermicelli**
> **2 carrots, cut into matchsticks**
> **2 cucumbers, cut into matchsticks**
> **1 red pepper, cut into matchsticks**
> **3 spring onions, cut into thin strips**
> **125 g/4 oz button mushrooms, quartered**
> **30 g/1 oz bean sprouts**
> **1 bunch fresh coriander**

chili and lime dressing

> **¹/4 cup/45 g/1¹/2 oz brown sugar**
> **1 clove garlic, crushed**
> **2 fresh red chilies, finely chopped**
> **¹/2 cup/125 ml/4 fl oz lime juice**
> **¹/4 cup/60 ml/2 fl oz fish sauce**

method

1. To make dressing, place sugar, garlic, chilies, lime juice and fish sauce in a bowl and whisk to combine.
2. Place vermicelli in a bowl, pour over boiling water to cover and soak for 10 minutes. Drain well and place in a serving bowl.
3. Add carrots, cucumbers, red pepper, spring onions, mushrooms, bean sprouts and coriander leaves. Pour over dressing and toss to combine. Cover and refrigerate for 2 hours before serving.

....

Serves 4

tip from the chef

When trying to cool your mouth down after eating chili-flavored foods, do not drink water or beer. While this cools the tongue it spreads the burning chili oil around the rest of your mouth and so makes the whole experience even more fiery. A glass of milk, a cool yogurt sambal or dip, or neutral foods such as plain bread, rice, noodles or mashed potatoes are the most effective mouth coolers and neutralizers.

avocado
sushi

■ ■ ■ | Cooking time: 18 minutes - Preparation time: 50 minutes

method

1. Combine rice and water in pan, bring to boil, reduce heat, simmer uncovered until water is absorbed. Cover pan, simmer 5 minutes. Stir in combined vinegar, sugar and salt.

2. Arrange nori sheets in single layer on oven tray. Toast in oven at 180°C/350°F/Gas 4 for 2 minutes or until crisp.

3. Cut a strip about 4 cm/1½ in wide from the narrow end of the nori sheet. Place the large piece of nori in the center of a bamboo mat, place the extra narrow strip in the center; this helps strengthen the nori during rolling.

4. Spread about a fifth of the rice over nori. At the end furthest away from you leave a 4 cm/1½ in edge. Make a hollow with wet fingers horizontally across the center. Spread the wasabi paste along hollow in rice. Place a combination of cucumber, avocado and ginger in hollow of rice.

5. Use bamboo mat to help roll the sushi, pressing firmly as you roll. Remove bamboo mat. Use a sharp knife to cut sushi into 4 cm/1½ in slices.

ingredients

> 2 cups short grain rice
> 3 cups water
> 5 sheets nori
> ⅓ cup rice vinegar
> ⅓ cup sugar
> 3 teaspoons salt
> 2 teaspoons wasabi paste
> 1 small green cucumber, peeled, seeded, cut into thin strips
> 1 avocado, peeled, cut into thin strips
> 60 g/2 oz packet sliced pickled ginger, cut into thin strips

Serves 4

tip from the chef

Nori, wasabi paste and pickled ginger are available from Asian food shops.

spicy pumpkin soup

■□□ I Cooking time: 8 minutes - Preparation time: 30 minutes

ingredients

> **2 tablespoons margarine**
> **1 large onion, chopped**
> **1 1/2 cups degreased chicken stock**
> **3 cups pumpkin purée**
> **1/4 teaspoon nutmeg**
> **1/2 cup non fat evaporated milk**

method

1. Heat margarine in a large saucepan over medium heat, add onion and cook for 2 minutes.
2. Add the stock, pumpkin purée and nutmeg. Simmer gently until mixture boils.
3. Stir in evaporated milk and serve immediately. Garnish with fresh chopped parsley if desired.

....

Serves 4

tip from the chef

To reduce even more the fatty content of this soup, margarine can be replaced by canola oil.

savory pumpkin flan

a

■ ■ □ | Cooking time: 35 minutes - Preparation time: 30 minutes

method

1. Brush each sheet of pastry with oil (a) and fold in half. Layer pastry, one folded piece on top of the other to give eight layers. Place an 18 cm/7 in flan dish upside down on layered pastry and cut around dish, making a circle 3 cm/1¼ in larger. Lift all layers of pastry into dish and roll edges.

2. Cook onion in a frying pan for 4-5 minutes or until onion is opaque and soft. Place pumpkin or carrots, cheese, egg yolks, sour cream or yogurt, chili powder and black pepper to taste in a bowl (b) and mix to combine.

3. Place egg whites in a bowl and beat until stiff peaks form. Fold egg white mixture into pumpkin mixture and spoon into pastry case (c). Sprinkle pumpkin mixture with parsley and bake at 150°C/300°F/Gas 2 for 30 minutes or until pastry is golden and cooked.

ingredients

> **4 sheets filo pastry**
> **2 tablespoons vegetable oil**
> **1 onion, chopped**
> **250 g/8 oz pumpkin or carrots, cooked and mashed**
> **185 g/6 oz grated tasty low fat cheese**
> **2 eggs, separated**
> **2 tablespoons natural low fat yogurt**
> **pinch chili powder**
> **freshly ground black pepper**
> **1 tablespoon chopped fresh parsley**

....

Serves 4

tip from the chef

When incorporating beaten egg whites into a mixture, first stir in 1 tablespoon of beaten egg white, then lightly fold remaining beaten egg white through, working as quickly as possible.

b

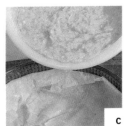

c

lettuce
roll-ups

■□□ | Cooking time: 0 minutes - Preparation time: 35 minutes

ingredients
> **6 large lettuce leaves**
> **1 cup/60 g bean sprouts**
> **2 mangoes, peeled and chopped**
> **260 g/9 oz canned sliced water chestnuts, drained**
> **2 teaspoons finely chopped preserved ginger**
> **2 teaspoons finely chopped mint leaves**
> **3 tablespoons low fat mayonnaise**
> **1 tablespoon low fat unflavored yogurt**

method
1. Tear lettuce leaves in half lengthways. Toss together sprouts, mangoes, water chestnuts, ginger and mint.
2. Combine mayonnaise and yogurt. Fold through mango mixture.
3. Place a spoonful of mixture on each lettuce leaf. Roll up tightly and secure with a toothpick.

....
Serves 6

tip from the chef
These rolls can also be made with blanched cabbage leaves, and stuffed with mashed carrots and tofu, seasoned with sesame oil and chopped chives.

fish and chippies

■□□ | Cooking time: 45 minutes - Preparation time: 15 minutes

method

1. Pat fish dry with absorbent kitchen paper and set aside.
2. Place garlic, dill, wine and lemon juice in a shallow glass or ceramic dish and mix to combine. Add fish, cover and marinate in the refrigerator for 2 hours.
3. Place potatoes on a nonstick baking tray, brush lightly with oil and bake at 220°C/425°F/Gas 7, turning several times, for 30-45 minutes or until potatoes are crisp and golden.
4. Drain fish well and cook under a preheated medium grill for 5 minutes or until fish flakes when tested with a fork. Serve immediately with potato wedges.

ingredients

> 4 firm white fish fillets
> 1 clove garlic, crushed
> 1 tablespoon chopped fresh dill
> 1/4 cup/60 ml/2 fl oz white wine
> 2 tablespoons lemon juice
> 4 large potatoes, cut into wedges
> 1 tablespoon olive oil

....
Serves 4

tip from the chef

Nearly all white meat sea fish, like sole, are lean. Freshwater fish, of yellowish meat, are fatter, the same as tuna fish.

fish parcels with mushroom sauce

■□□ | Cooking time: 25 minutes - Preparation time: 25 minutes

ingredients

> **4 gemfish fillets,
125 g/4 oz each**
> **2 tablespoons lemon juice**
> **12 sheets filo pastry**
> **1/4 cup melted margarine**

mushroom sauce

> **1 1/2 tablespoon
cornflour**
> **1/2 cup cold degreased
chicken stock**
> **3/4 cup skim milk**
> **1 1/2 cups button
mushrooms, sliced**
> **pinch nutmeg**

method

1. Lightly season fish with salt and pepper, brush with lemon juice (a).
2. Divide filo into four piles, 3 sheets in each. Brush margarine (b) between each sheet.
3. Place fish fillet on each pile of filo and roll each one up into a parcel (c), tucking in ends.
4. Place fish parcels seamside down on a greased baking tray (d). Bake at 180°C/350°F/Gas 4 for 20 minutes.
5. To make sauce, combine cornflour with chicken stock to make a thin paste. Add the milk and pour into a small saucepan. Heat gently, stirring constantly, until sauce begins to thicken, add mushrooms and nutmeg, cook a further 3 minutes. Serve sauce over parcels.

....
Serves 4

tip from the chef

The mushroom sauce can be replaced by a mushroom and watercress salad, dressed with lemon juice and extra virgin olive oil.

a

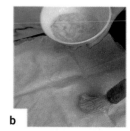

b

salmon with
pepper and mint

■□□ | Cooking time: 6 minutes - Preparation time: 15 minutes

method

1. To make marinade, place wine, lime juice, mint and black pepper in a large shallow glass or ceramic dish and mix to combine.
2. Add salmon to marinade and set aside to marinate for 10 minutes. Turn once. Drain and cook on a preheated hot barbecue or under a grill for 2-3 minutes each side or until salmon flakes when tested with a fork. Serve immediately.

Serves 4

ingredients

> **4 salmon cutlets**

pepper and mint marinade

> **3 tablespoons dry white wine**
> **2 tablespoons lime juice**
> **2 tablespoons chopped fresh mint**
> **2 teaspoons crushed black peppercorns**

tip from the chef

Nothing like crispy potato chips to complement your fish dish. To give them a tempting aroma, sprinkle potato wedges with salt and rosemary before baking until crisp and golden.

stir-fried
vegetable and seafood

■ ■ □ | Cooking time: 10 minutes - Preparation time: 25 minutes

ingredients

> 2 squid tubes
> 2 tablespoons olive oil
> 1 teaspoon sesame oil
> 1 onion, sliced
> 1/2 red pepper, sliced
> 1/2 yellow pepper, sliced
> 100 g/3 1/2 oz snow peas
> 200 g/7 oz scallops
> 200 g/7 oz uncooked
  prawns, shelled and
  deveined
> 2 tablespoons soy sauce
> salt
> freshly ground black
  pepper

method

1. Using a sharp knife, make a single cut down the length of each squid tube and open out. Cut parallel lines down the length of the squid, taking care not to cut right the way through the flesh. Make more cuts in the opposite direction to form a diamond pattern.
2. Heat oils in a deep frying pan and stir-fry onion for 2 minutes. Add red and yellow pepper, snow peas and squid. Stir-fry for 5 minutes or until vegetables are tender.
3. Add scallops, prawns and soy sauce. Season with salt and black pepper to taste and cook for 2 minutes more.

....

Serves 4

tip from the chef

This dish is delicious when seasoned with fresh thyme leaves and sesame seeds. Add the seeds at the moment of serving so they will be crisp. Also, include other seafood and fish, cut into strips, for variation.

scallops and wilted spinach

■☐☐ | Cooking time: 3 minutes - Preparation time: 10 minutes

method

1. Preheat barbecue to a medium heat.
2. To make salad, blanch spinach leaves in boiling water for 10 seconds. Drain spinach, refresh under cold running water, drain again and place in a bowl.
3. Place sesame seeds, soy sauce, lemon juice and sesame oil in a bowl and mix to combine. Spoon dressing over spinach and toss to combine. Divide salad between serving plates.
4. Place scallops in bowl, drizzle with a little vegetable oil and season to taste with black pepper. Sear scallops on barbecue plate for 45-60 seconds or until golden and flesh is opaque. Place scallops on top of each salad and serve immediately.

....
Serves 6

ingredients

> **18 scallops**
> **vegetable oil**
> **crushed black peppercorns**

wilted spinach salad

> **185 g/6 oz baby English spinach leaves**
> **2 teaspoons sesame seeds**
> **2 tablespoons soy sauce**
> **1 tablespoon lemon juice**
> **2 teaspoons sesame oil**

tip from the chef
Alternatively the scallops can be seared in a hot frying pan.

herbed chicken
and tomato casserole

■□□ I Cooking time: 25 minutes - Preparation time: 25 minutes

ingredients

> 2 tablespoons safflower oil
> 1 small onion, peeled and sliced
> 1 green pepper, seeds removed, cut into strips
> 1 red pepper, seeds removed, cut into strips
> 1 zucchini, sliced
> 1½ cups tomato purée
> 1 tablespoon chopped fresh basil
> 1 tablespoon chopped fresh parsley
> 1 teaspoon chopped fresh thyme
> 3 chicken breast fillets, 125 g/4oz each, fat and skin removed, cut into strips

method

1. In a large frying pan over medium heat, heat the oil and add onion (a). Cook until transparent.
2. Add green and red peppers, zucchini and tomato purée (b). Bring to the boil, reduce heat and simmer for 10 minutes.
3. Add the basil, parsley, thyme and chicken (c), cook for 10 minutes or until chicken is cooked through.

....

Serves 4

tip from the chef

After fish, the leanest meats are turkey, duck and chicken.

a

b

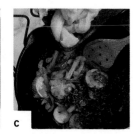
c

italian
chicken salad

■□□ | Cooking time: 12 minutes - Preparation time: 25 minutes

method

1. Heat a nonstick char-grill or frying pan over a high heat. Lightly spray chicken with olive oil, add to pan and cook for 2-3 minutes each side or until tender. Remove from pan and set aside to cool.
2. To make dressing, place prunes, oregano, lemon rind, sugar and vinegar in a saucepan over a low heat, bring to simmering and simmer for 5 minutes.
3. To assemble salad, cut chicken breasts into thin slices. Arrange spinach, beans, onion, chicken and capers attractively on serving plates. Drizzle a little warm dressing over the salad and serve immediately. Serve any remaining dressing separately.

....

Serves 4

ingredients

> **2 boneless chicken breast fillets, all visible fat and skin removed**
> **olive oil spray**
> **125 g/4 oz baby English spinach leaves**
> **125 g/4 oz green beans, blanched**
> **1 red onion, thinly sliced**
> **2 tablespoons small capers, drained**

vinegar and prune dressing

> **8 pitted prunes**
> **1 tablespoon fresh oregano leaves**
> **shredded rind of 1 lemon**
> **1 teaspoon sugar**
> **1/2 cup/125 ml/4 fl oz red wine vinegar**

tip from the chef
Breast is the leanest part of the chicken.

chicken and
pepper tortillas

■■□ | Cooking time: 20 minutes - Preparation time: 40 minutes

ingredients

tortillas
> 7^1/$_2$ cups fine cornmeal
> 1^1/$_2$ cups plain flour
> pinch salt
> 75 g/2^1/$_2$ oz margarine, chopped
> ^{3}/$_4$ cup warm water

topping
> ^{1}/$_4$ cup tomato paste
> 100 g/3^1/$_2$ oz low fat cheese, grated
> 1 cup cooked chicken breast, chopped
> 2 tablespoons chopped green pepper
> 2 teaspoon chopped red chili

method

1. Mix cornmeal, flour and salt together in a medium bowl (a). Rub in margarine until mixture resembles fine breadcrumbs (b).
2. Add the water and mix to a dough. Lightly knead (c) on a floured surface for 2 minutes.
3. Roll dough out and using a 9 cm/3^1/$_2$ in round cutter, cut out 8 circles (d).
4. Place tortillas on a greased baking tray and bake at 180°C/350°F/Gas 4 for 10 minutes.
5. Spread tomato paste over each tortilla, sprinkle with cheese, chicken, green pepper and chili. Bake for 10 minutes more.

....
Makes 8 to 10

tip from the chef
Tortillas can be replaced by crêpes made with wholemeal flour and self-raising flour, in the proportion of 1 cup wholemeal every 2 cups self-raising flour.

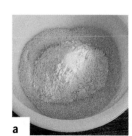
a

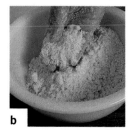
b

c

d

chicken and
asparagus rolls

■☐☐ I Cooking time: 8 minutes - Preparation time: 25 minutes

method

1. Boil, steam or microwave asparagus until just tender. Drain and set aside to cool.
2. Place chicken and chutney in a bowl and mix to combine. Top pitta bread with chicken mixture, asparagus, cucumber and green pepper. Roll up.

Serves 2

ingredients

> **250 g/8 oz asparagus spears**
> **125 g/4 oz chopped cooked chicken, all skin and visible fat removed**
> **1 tablespoon tomato chutney**
> **2 large wholemeal pitta bread rounds**
> **1/2 cucumber, sliced**
> **1/2 green pepper, sliced**

tip from the chef

If tomato chutney is unavailable, use a mixture of equal parts of ketchup, vinegar and peach or apricot jam.

chicken
mango pockets

■□□ I Cooking time: 0 minutes - Preparation time: 20 minutes

ingredients
- > **4 wholemeal pitta bread rounds**
- > **90 g/3 oz low fat ricotta cheese**
- > **1 small cucumber, chopped**
- > **2 tablespoons chopped fresh mint**
- > **1 teaspoon ground cumin**
- > **1 red onion, thinly sliced**
- > **90 g/3 oz alfalfa sprouts**
- > **500 g/1 lb cooked chicken, skin removed and flesh shredded**
- > **4 tablespoons mango chutney**

method
1. Make a slit in the top of each pitta bread round. Set aside.
2. Place ricotta cheese, cucumber, mint and cumin in a bowl and mix to combine. Spread the inside of each pitta bread with ricotta mixture, then fill with onion, alfalfa sprouts, chicken and chutney.

....
Serves 4

tip from the chef
These pockets are fun and ideal for an outdoor brunch.

turkey muffins

■□□ | Cooking time: 5 minutes - Preparation time: 10 minutes

method

1. Place tomato slices on muffin halves. Top with turkey slices, cheese and black pepper to taste.
2. Place under a preheated grill until heated through.

Serves 2

ingredients

> 2 muffins, halved and toasted

topping

> 1 tomato, sliced
> 2 slices cooked turkey breast
> 3 tablespoons grated low fat tasty cheese
> freshly ground black pepper

tip from the chef

These muffins will have a touch of Mediterranean flavor if you use dried tomatoes instead of fresh ones and add a few basil leaves.

spicy veal skewers

■□□ I Cooking time: 5 minutes - Preparation time: 25 minutes

ingredients

> **500 g/1 lb veal fillet, trimmed of visible fat and cut into thin strips**

coconut and coriander marinade

> **2 tablespoons chopped fresh coriander**
> **1 tablespoon red curry paste**
> **1/3 cup/90 ml/3 fl oz reduced fat coconut milk**

method

1. Thread veal strips onto lightly oiled skewers.
2. To make marinade, place coriander, curry paste and coconut milk in a bowl and mix to combine. Brush marinade over veal and marinate for 20 minutes.
3. Heat a nonstick char-grill pan over a high heat, add veal skewers and cook for 1-2 minutes each side or until tender.

Serves 4

tip from the chef

These skewers can also be cooked on the barbecue or under a preheated grill.

steaks
in wine marinade

■ □ □ | Cooking time: 10 minutes - Preparation time: 10 minutes

method

1. To make marinade, place garlic, red wine, sugar and black pepper to taste in a shallow glass or ceramic dish. Add steaks, turn to coat and marinate for 5 minutes. Turn over and marinate for 5 minutes longer. Drain steaks and reserve marinade.

2. Heat oil in a frying pan over a high heat, add steaks and cook for 1-2 minutes each side or until cooked to your liking. Remove steaks from pan, set aside and keep warm. Add reserved marinade to pan and boil until reduced by half. Spoon sauce over steaks and serve immediately.

ingredients

> 4 lean veal or pork steaks
> 1 tablespoon vegetable oil

red wine marinade

> 2 cloves garlic, crushed
> 1/4 cup/185 ml/6 fl oz red wine
> 3 tablespoons brown sugar
> freshly ground black pepper

Serves 4

tip from the chef

Serve with peppered fettuccine and vegetables. For fettuccine, toss hot fettuccine with 1 tablespoon olive oil and 1 tablespoon coarsely crushed black peppercorns.

beef
and pasta bake

■ ■ □ | Cooking time: 50 minutes - Preparation time: 30 minutes

ingredients

> 1 onion, chopped
> 2 cloves garlic, crushed
> 1 teaspoon ground cumin
> 500 g/1 lb lean minced beef
> 2 tablespoons chopped fresh mint
> 2 x 440 g/14 oz canned tomatoes, undrained and mashed
> 1/2 cup/125 ml/4 fl oz degreased beef stock
> 2 eggplant, sliced
> 12 sheets instant (no precooking required) lasagna

ricotta topping

> 155 g/5 oz low fat ricotta cheese, drained
> 2 tablespoons chopped fresh marjoram or oregano
> freshly ground black pepper

method

1. Place onion, garlic and cumin in a nonstick frying pan over a high heat and cook, stirring, for 5 minutes or until onion is golden.

2. Add beef and cook, stirring, for 5 minutes or until meat is brown. Add mint, tomatoes and stock, bring to simmering and simmer, stirring occasionally, for 10 minutes.

3. Layer eggplant, beef mixture and lasagna sheets in a lightly greased ovenproof dish, finishing with a layer of eggplant.

4. To make topping, place ricotta cheese, marjoram or oregano and black pepper to taste in a bowl and mix to combine. Spread topping over eggplant and bake at 180°C/350°F/Gas 4 for 30 minutes or until eggplant and pasta are tender and top is golden.

....

Serves 4

tip from the chef

When using instant (no precooking required) lasagna, the cooked dish tends to be moister and the pasta more tender if the lasagna sheets are dipped in warm water before assembling the dish.

lamb with
roast pepper purée

■□□ | Cooking time: 25 minutes - Preparation time: several hours

method

1. Place garlic, wine, vinegar, mustard and honey in a shallow glass or ceramic dish and mix to combine. Add lamb, cover and marinate in the refrigerator for 3-4 hours or overnight.

2. To make purée, place red and yellow peppers, skin side up, under a preheated hot grill and cook for 10-15 minutes or until skins are blistered and charred. Place peppers in a plastic food bag or paper bag and set aside until cool enough to handle, then remove skins. Place peppers and yogurt in a food processor or blender and process to make a purée. Stir in mint and set aside.

3. Drain lamb and cook under a preheated medium grill or on a barbecue for 3-5 minutes each side or until lamb is cooked to your liking. Serve with purée.

ingredients

> 1 clove garlic, crushed
> 1/4 cup/60 ml/2 fl oz white wine
> 2 tablespoons tarragon vinegar
> 2 tablespoons wholegrain mustard
> 1 tablespoon honey
> 8 lamb cutlets, trimmed of all visible fat

roast pepper purée

> 1 red pepper, seeded and quartered
> 1 yellow pepper, seeded and quartered
> 1/2 cup/100 g/3 1/2 oz natural low fat yogurt
> 2 tablespoons chopped fresh mint

Serves 4

tip from the chef

This very elaborate dish is excellent for dinner parties. The pepper sauce can be enhanced with sage leaves.

pork with
orange and cranberry

■□□ I Cooking time: 15 minutes - Preparation time: several hours

ingredients

> **4 x 125 g/4 oz lean butterfly pork steaks**
> **cracked black peppercorns**
> **1 teaspoon grape seed oil**

marinade

> **1 cup/250 ml/8 fl oz fresh orange juice**
> **2 teaspoons grated orange rind**
> **¹/4 teaspoon ground cloves**
> **3 tablespoons cranberry sauce**

method

1. Trim all visible fat from meat. To make marinade, combine orange juice, orange rind, cloves and cranberry sauce in a glass bowl. Add meat and marinate for 1-2 hours.
2. Remove steaks from marinade and coat with peppercorns. Heat oil in a nonstick frying pan. Cook steaks for 4-5 minutes each side or until cooked. Set aside and keep warm.
3. Strain remaining marinade and pour into a saucepan. Bring to the boil and boil rapidly to reduce slightly. Spoon sauce over steaks and serve.

....
Serves 4

tip from the chef
Butterfly pork steaks, with their lean meaty quality, are excellent with this tasty sauce.

quinces with honey yogurt

■□□ | Cooking time: 40 minutes - Preparation time: 20 minutes

method

1. Place water and sugar in a large saucepan and cook over a low heat, stirring constantly, until sugar dissolves.
2. Add lemon rind and quinces to syrup, bring to the boil and simmer for 40 minutes or until quinces are tender and change color.
3. To serve, place quinces on serving plates, spoon over a little of the cooking liquid, accompany with yogurt and drizzle with honey.

ingredients

> **6 cups/1.5 liters/2¹/2 pt water**
> **1¹/2 cups/375 g/12 oz sugar**
> **4 strips lemon rind**
> **6 quinces, peeled and quartered**
> **3/4 cup/185 ml/6 fl oz natural low fat yogurt**
> **3 tablespoons honey**

···········
Serves 6

tip from the chef

If quinces are unavailable, this recipe is also good when made with apples or pears. The cooking time will not be so long.

berry-filled
tea pancakes

■■□ | Cooking time: 30 minutes - Preparation time: 35 minutes

ingredients

pancakes
> 100 g/3 oz plain flour, sifted
> 1 egg, lightly beaten
> 1 cup/250 ml/8 fl oz cold tea
> 1 tablespoon polyunsaturated oil
> 2 tablespoons icing sugar, sifted

filling
> 1 cup/250 g/8 oz low fat ricotta cheese
> 1 cup/250 g/8 oz low fat unflavored yogurt
> 2 tablespoons rosewater
> 100 g/3 oz fresh strawberries, hulled and halved
> 100 g/3 oz raspberries
> 2 kiwi fruit, sliced

method

1. To make pancakes, place flour in a bowl and make a well in the center. Add egg and work flour in from the sides. Stir in tea a little at a time to make a smooth batter of pouring consistency. Set aside to stand for 30 minutes before cooking.
2. Pour 2 tablespoons batter into a lightly greased nonstick frying pan. Cook pancakes until golden brown each side.
3. To make filling, place ricotta, yogurt and rosewater in food processor or blender. Process until smooth. Transfer to a bowl and fold through fruit. To serve, divide filling between pancakes. Roll up and dust with icing sugar.

....
Makes 10

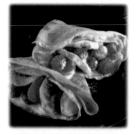

tip from the chef
These pancakes are great if accompanied with iced tea. To make tea, place 4 cups/ 1 liter/1 3/4 pt cold water and 4 tea bags in a large glass jug. Cover and refrigerate overnight. To serve, place ice cubes in a long glass, pour in tea and garnish with lemon slices.

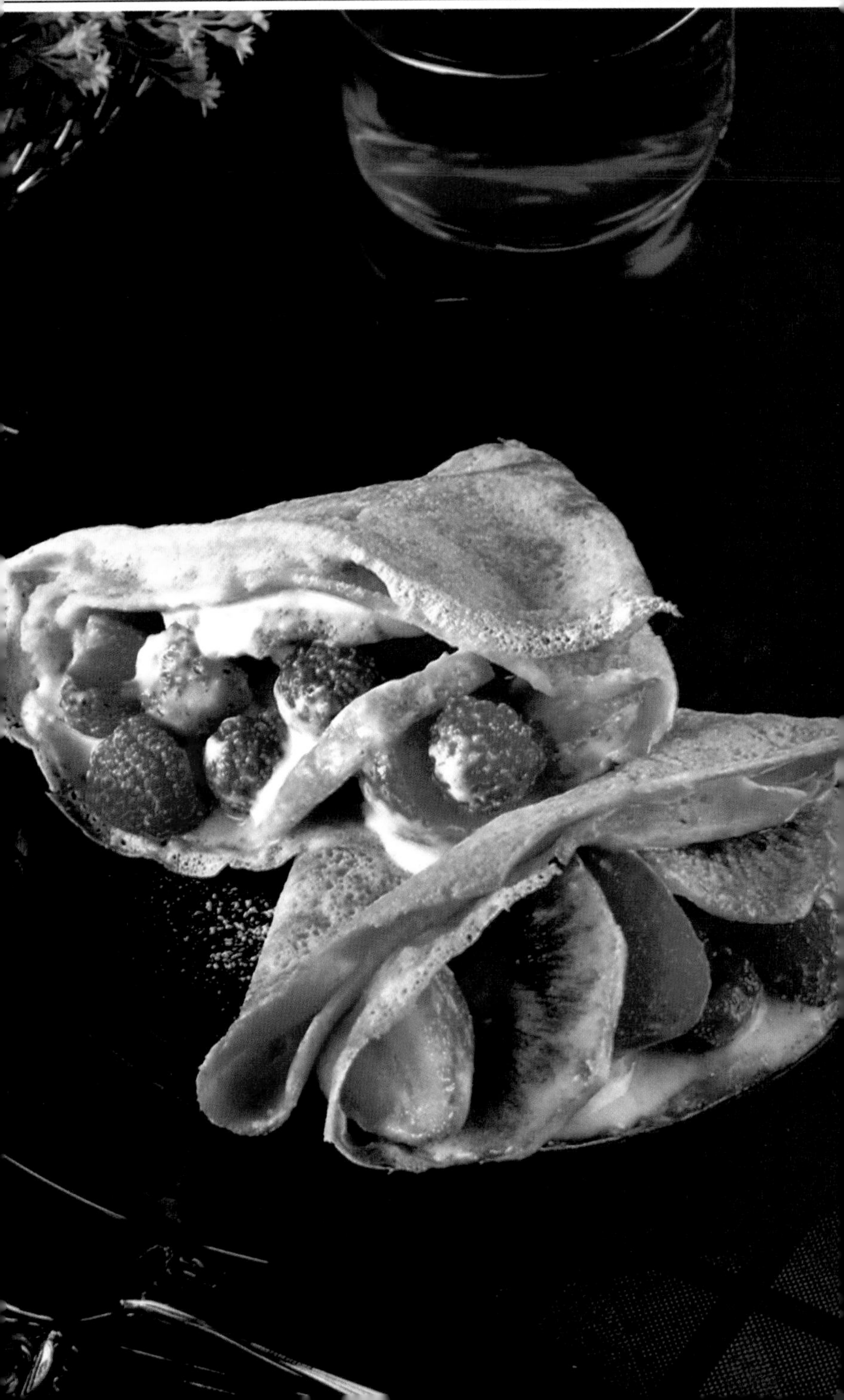

mixed berry meringues with apricot coulis

■ ■ □ | Cooking time: 45 minutes - Preparation time: 30 minutes

method

1. Beat egg whites with electric mixer until light and fluffy. Slowly add sugar while motor is running.
2. Add vanilla and beat for a further 10 minutes until mixture is thick and glossy.
3. Place mixture into a piping bag and pipe nests approximately 6 cm/2¹/₂ in diameter onto a greased paper-lined baking tray.
4. Bake at 160°C/325°F/Gas 3 for 20 minutes, reduce heat to 120°C/250°F/Gas 1 and bake for a further 25 minutes.
5. In a small bowl combine raspberries, blueberries and Grand Marnier and place berries in the center of meringue nests.
6. In a food processor or blender, process apricot halves with apricot nectar until smooth. Spoon 2 tablespoons of this apricot coulis onto each serving plate, place meringue nest in center of coulis. Decorate with fresh sprig of mint if desired.

ingredients

> **3 egg whites, at room temperature**
> **¹/₃ cup caster sugar**
> **1 teaspoon vanilla essence**
> **¹/₂ cup raspberries**
> **¹/₂ cup blueberries**
> **3 tablespoons Grand Marnier**
> **1 cup canned apricot halves, drained**
> **¹/₄ cup apricot nectar**

....
Serves 4-6

tip from the chef
Egg whites are fat free and rich in protein. They are a must in low fat diets.

yogurt
orange ice cream

■ ■ ■ | Cooking time: 0 minutes - Preparation time: several hours

method

1. Combine the honey and yogurt in a large bowl (a); mix well. Dissolve gelatin in the water (b). Cool slightly, then stir into yogurt mixture (c).
2. Line a loaf tin with cling film. Spoon yogurt mixture into the tin, cover and freeze for 3 hours.
3. Beat the frozen mixture in a large bowl until doubled in bulk. Beat in the vanilla, orange rind and juice.
4. Whisk the egg whites to soft peaks in a separate, grease-free bowl. Fold into the yogurt ice, return the mixture to the loaf tin, cover and freeze until solid. Soften slightly before serving with fresh fruit.

ingredients

> 4 tablespoons clear honey
> 375 ml/12 fl oz orange-flavored low fat yogurt
> 1 tablespoon gelatin
> 60 ml/2 fl oz hot water
> 1 teaspoon vanilla essence
> 2 teaspoons finely grated orange rind
> 2 tablespoons freshly squeezed orange juice
> 2 egg whites

....
Serves 6-8

tip from the chef

A deliciously surprising ice cream can be made if saffron tea is used instead of orange juice.

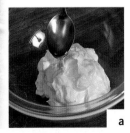
a

b

c

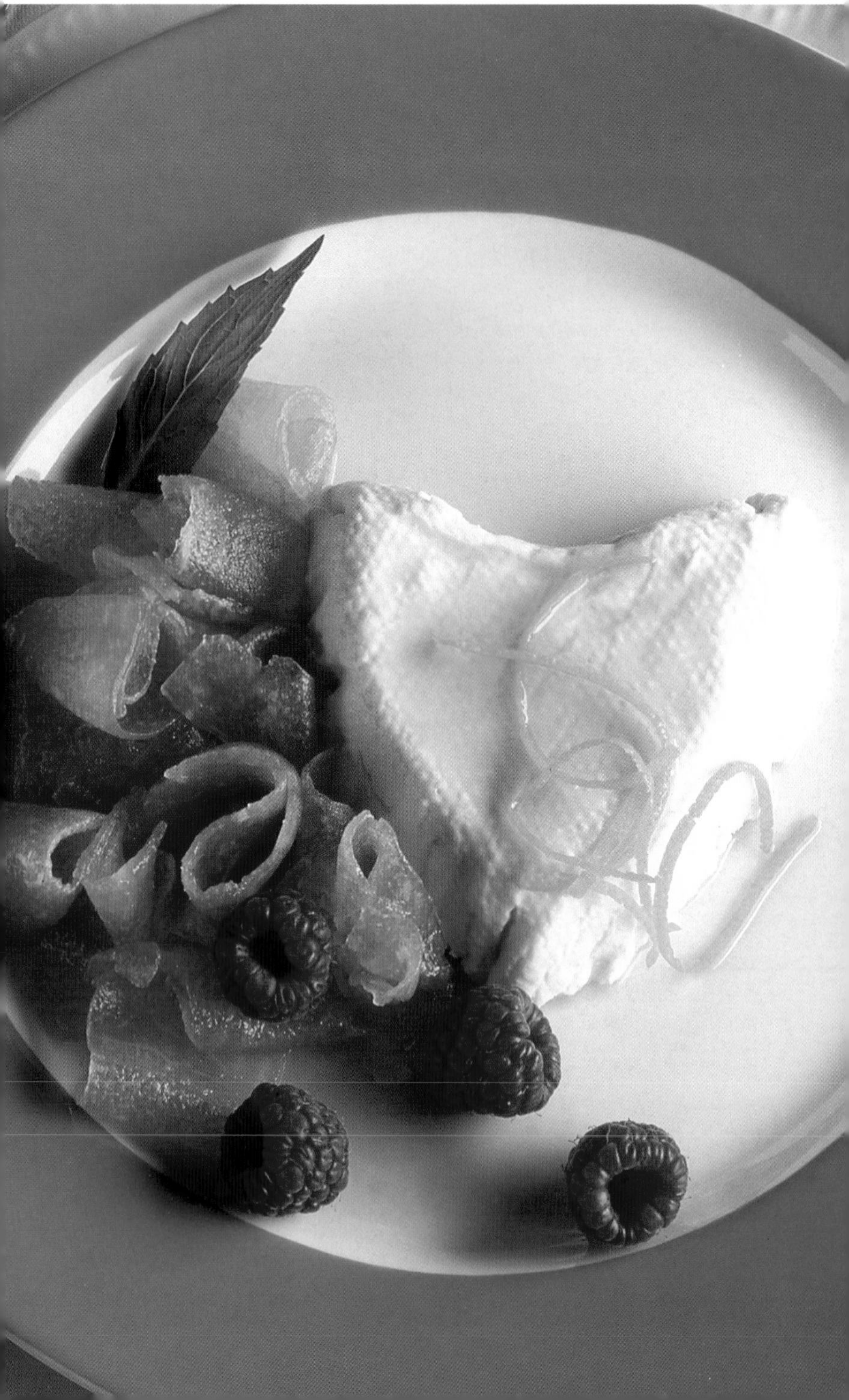

cœur
à la crème

■□□ | Cooking time: 0 minutes - Preparation time: 10 minutes

method

1. Place cottage cheese in a food processor or blender and process until smooth. Add cream cheese, icing sugar, cream and vanilla essence and process to combine.
2. Line four cœur à la crème molds with a double thickness of damp muslin or gauze and pack cheese mixture into molds. Place molds on a wire rack, on a tray. Cover and refrigerate for 24 hours. Turn crèmes onto serving plates, sprinkle each with a little liqueur and garnish with fruit.

ingredients

- > **185 g/6 oz cottage cheese**
- > **60 g/2 oz reduced fat cream cheese**
- > **1 tablespoon icing sugar**
- > **1/4 cup/60 ml/2 fl oz cream (light)**
- > **1/2 teaspoon vanilla essence**
- > **1 tablespoon orange-flavored liqueur**
- > **250 g/8 oz mixed fruits, such as berries of your choice, plums, peaches or melons**

....
Serves 4

tip from the chef

Start preparing this dessert the day before serving as it has to sit in the refrigerator overnight.
Cœur à la crème molds are china, heart-shaped molds with draining holes in the base. Before lining with the muslin you should rinse them in cold water, but do not dry. You can make your own molds, using small empty plastic containers. Cut the containers down to make sides of about 2.5 cm/1 in, then, using a skewer, punch holes in the base. These molds will not be heart-shaped like the traditional ones but the dessert will still look and taste wonderful.

wholemeal
date scones

■ ■ □ I Cooking time: 15 minutes - Preparation time: 30 minutes

ingredients
> **1 cup wholemeal self-raising flour**
> **1 cup white self-raising flour**
> **1 cup unprocessed bran**
> **60 g/2 oz margarine**
> **125 g/4 oz dates, finely chopped**
> **1 cup skim milk**

method
1. Sift flours into bowl, return husks from sifter to bowl, mix in bran. Rub in margarine, add dates.
2. Make well in center of dry ingredients, stir in enough milk to give a soft, sticky dough.
3. Turn dough onto lightly floured surface and knead lightly until smooth. Press dough out to 1 cm/1/2 in thickness, cut into rounds with 5 cm/2 in cutter.
4. Place scones into greased slab tin, bake at 180°C/350°F/Gas 4 15 minutes or until golden brown.

....
Makes about 15

tip from the chef
These wholemeal scones are perfect for an afternoon tea or for a full breakfast.

lemon
cheesecake

■□□ | Cooking time: 45 minutes - Preparation time: 15 minutes

method

1. Place cottage and ricotta cheeses, sugar, yogurt and eggs in a food processor and process until smooth. Add cornflour and lemon rind and process to combine.

2. Pour mixture into a lightly greased 23 cm/9 in round cake tin and place in a baking dish with enough water to come halfway up the sides of the tin. Bake at 150°C/300°F/Gas 2 for 45 minutes or until cake is firm to touch. Cool cheesecake in tin.

....

Serves 10

ingredients

> 2 cups/500 g/1 lb low fat cottage cheese, drained
> 1 cup/250 g/8 oz low fat ricotta cheese, drained
> 1/3 cup/90 g/3 oz sugar
> 1 cup/200 g/6 1/2 oz thick natural low fat yogurt
> 2 eggs
> 1/4 cup/30 g/1 oz cornflour
> 1 tablespoon finely grated lemon rind

tip from the chef

Cut cheesecake into wedges and accompany with fresh seasonal fruit. For a lime or orange version of this delicious dessert, replace the lemon rind with lime or orange rind.

country apple flan

■ ■ ■ | Cooking time: 45 minutes - Preparation time: 90 minutes

ingredients

pastry
> **1¹/2 cups plain flour**
> **¹/4 teaspoon salt**
> **³/4 teaspoon dry yeast**
> **³/4 cup warm water**

filling
> **2 tablespoons honey**
> **3 green apples, cored, peeled and thinly sliced**
> **2 teaspoons cinnamon sugar**
> **2 tablespoons brown sugar**

tip from the chef

Easy, low calorie alternative: briefly boil the apples in lemon juice. Place them in a lightly oiled pie dish and cover them with equal parts of rolled oats, brown sugar and beaten egg whites. Bake until golden.

method

1. Combine flour and salt in a large bowl. In a separate small bowl mix the yeast with the warm water (a) and let stand until yeast has dissolved, approximately 4 minutes.
2. Make a well in the center of flour mixture, pour in yeast mixture gradually while stirring in flour.
3. Knead dough (b) until smooth and elastic, approximately 10 minutes. Place dough in a large bowl, cover with a tea towel (c) and leave for 1 hour, in a warm place, to double in size.
4. Punch down dough, and leave to rise again for 30 minutes.
5. Roll out dough to fit a 23 cm/9 in flan dish and bake blind at 180°C/350°F/Gas 4 for 15 minutes.
6. Brush honey over pastry, arrange apple slices on top and sprinkle with combined cinnamon sugar and brown sugar. Bake for 30 minutes.

....
Serves 12

a

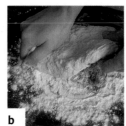

b

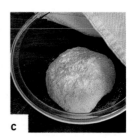

c

index